step-by-step
fast & simple

step-by-step
fast & simple

a visual step-by-step cookbook

This edition published in 2011
LOVE FOOD is an imprint of Parragon Books Ltd

Parragon
Queen Street House
4 Queen Street
Bath BA1 1HE, UK

ISBN: 978-1-4454-3656-2

Printed in China

Designed by Talking Design
Photography by Mike Cooper
Food styling by Lincoln Jefferson
New recipes by Christine France
Introduction by Linda Doeser

Notes for the Reader

This book uses imperial, metric, and US cup measurements. Follow the same units of measurement throughout; do not mix imperial and metric. All spoon measurements are level: teaspoons are assumed to be 5 ml, and tablespoons are assumed to be 15 ml. Unless otherwise stated, milk is assumed to be whole, eggs and individual vegetables, such as potatoes, are medium, and pepper is freshly ground black pepper.

The times given are an approximate guide only. Preparation times differ according to the techniques used by different people and the cooking times may also vary from those given as a result of the type of oven used. Optional ingredients, variations, or serving suggestions have not been included in the calculations.

Recipes using raw or very lightly cooked eggs should be avoided by infants, the elderly, pregnant women, convalescents, and anyone with a chronic condition. Pregnant and breast-feeding women are advised to avoid eating peanuts and peanut products. People with nut allergies should be aware that some of the prepared ingredients used in the recipes in this book may contain nuts. Always check the packaging before use. Vegetarians should be aware that some of the prepared ingredients used in the recipes in this book may contain animal products. Always check the packaging before use.

contents

introduction

This superb cookbook, with its wealth of beautiful and immensely useful photographs, will prove to be an invaluable addition to any cook's bookshelf. The recipes are clear, easy to follow, beautifully illustrated, and temptingly tasty, so whatever your level of expertise in the kitchen you are virtually guaranteed success every time.

Every recipe starts with a photograph of all the ingredients, but this is more than just a pretty picture or—even less helpful—a montage that is not to scale so that a chile pepper appears to be the same size as a whole fish. Instead, it serves as a handy way of checking that you have everything ready before you start cooking. Just comparing the picture with the ingredients arranged on your own counter or kitchen table will make sure that you haven't forgotten anything and when it's time to add the garlic, for example, you have already chopped it as specified in the ingredients list. If you're uncertain about how small to dice fruit or how finely to crush cookies, a glance at the photograph will provide an instant answer.

Each short and straightforward step of the method is clearly explained without any jargon or difficult technical terms. Once again, what you see in the photograph is what you should expect to see in front of you. Not only is this reassuring for the novice cook, but those with more experience will find it a helpful reminder of the little touches that can easily be overlooked. Each recipe ends with a photograph of the finished dish, complete with any serving suggestions.

Why you need this book

Eating well is one of the primary keys to good health for you and your family, yet the pace of modern life is often frantic and time is limited. No one really wants or can afford to spend hours in the kitchen and, equally important, no one wants to struggle trying to understand a complicated recipe that somehow always turns out to be disappointing and not at all what they expected.

In this book there are 60 fuss-free recipes for delicious dishes for all occasions and every taste, from succulent stir-fried beef to elegant glazed duck and from spicy seafood stew to great vegetarian dishes, as well wonderfully self-indulgent desserts. All of them take less than half an hour to prepare and many can be made in just minutes.

top tips for fast and simple cooking

> Read all the way through the recipe—ingredients list and method—before you start so that you know exactly what you will need. Scrabbling about at the back of the pantry to find a rarely used ingredient or moving half a dozen other utensils to reach the one you need in the middle of cooking a dish is, at best, exasperating and, at worst, liable to cause the dish you are cooking to burn.

> Ovens and broilers take time to heat up so, if you are going to use either of them, turn them on as soon as you go into the kitchen. Fan-assisted ovens do not usually require preheating, but conventional ovens can take 15 minutes to reach the specified temperature. If the recipe calls for hot water, put it on to boil in advance.

> Collect all your ingredients together and make sure that they are ready to use—vegetables peeled or washed, for example. In addition, do any initial preparation described in the ingredients list, such as chopping onions. Check the photograph.

> Arrange the plates and bowls of ingredients in the order in which they are to be used. If a number of ingredients, such as flavorings and spices, are to be added at the same time, put them in small piles on the same plate.

> As you finish using utensils, move them out of your way. A cluttered counter is the enemy of speed and efficiency and can be dangerous.

> Be realistic about how much time you have and what you can reasonably handle. There's no point in cooking the main course in a flash if the vegetables you intended to accompany it take a lot longer. Consider a no-cook dessert or an appetizer that can be prepared in advance if the main course requires your undivided attention.

> Take advantage of convenience foods, such as bags of diced vegetables, trimmed and washed leeks, bottled pesto, canned beans and tomatoes, and jars of shredded garlic, ginger, and chiles. These will be more expensive than ingredients you need to prepare yourself, so strike a balance between cost and saving time. Remember that some convenience foods come at the price of flavor and are not really worth buying.

time-saving shortcuts

> Not all vegetables, including potatoes, have to be peeled before cooking. Most of the nutrients are often found just under the skin, so it is better simply to scrub them. After cooking, they can be peeled if necessary, or, if very young, they can be served as they are. Thin-skinned vegetables, such as zucchini and eggplants, do not need peeling at all. "Old" vegetables do need to be peeled and so too do carrots, even young ones, because they have a tendency to retain agricultural chemicals just beneath the skin.

> The easiest way to peel tomatoes, nectarines, peaches, and shallots is to put them into a heatproof bowl and pour over boiling water to cover. Let stand for 30–60 seconds and drain. The skins will slip off much more easily. Tomatoes and peaches will be even easier to peel if you slit the skins first.

> To peel a garlic clove, lightly crush it by pressing down with the flat blade of a cook's knife. The skin can then be removed easily and the garlic can be chopped, sliced, or, quickest of all, crushed with a garlic press.

> Some ingredients—cured ham, bacon, some fresh herbs, and dried fruit, for example—are much easier and quicker to snip into pieces with scissors rather than dice with a knife. Trim green beans and snow peas with kitchen scissors, too.

> Don't bother to peel avocados if you're going to mash or process the flesh. Simply halve and pit, then scoop out the flesh with a teaspoon.

> To coat cubes of meat in flour before browning, put the flour into a plastic bag and add the cubes a few at a time. Hold the bag closed and shake gently until the meat is coated. Repeat until finished.

> When slicing soft cheese, such as Camembert, dampen the blade of the knife to prevent the slices from sticking.

> To seed bell peppers, halve them lengthwise and cut out the membranes, together with most of the seeds, with a small knife. Turn the halves over and tap sharply on a cutting board so that any remaining seeds fall out.

> Melt chocolate in the microwave oven. Break it into pieces and put it into a microwave-proof bowl. Heat on MEDIUM for 10 seconds, then stir. Return to the microwave and heat for an additional 10 seconds before checking and stirring again—even when it's melted it will hold its shape, so you cannot tell if it's ready by just looking at it. White chocolate should be heated on LOW.

> If you have any leftover fresh breadcrumbs or grated cheese, divide into portions and freeze for another day. These make the perfect quick topping for gratins and casseroles.

> Leftover wine can also be frozen. Freeze it in an ice-cube tray and the next time you're cooking a casserole, you can pop in a cube or two to add extra depth of flavor.

> When you are using the food processor to chop vegetables, such as onions, make extra and store in sealed plastic bags in the refrigerator, ready to use as and when you need them during the week.

useful equipment

> **Wok:** Stir-frying is one of the fastest techniques for cooking food. The principle is simple: Ingredients are cut, sliced, or chopped into small, even-size pieces and then stirred over a very high heat in a small amount of oil for a brief period until cooked through and tender.

A wok is basically a gently sloping conical pan designed for constant stirring, so that food moves continually back to the center where the heat is most intense. Those with a round bottom work well on gas stovetops, while flat-bottom woks are designed for electric and ceramic stoves. Some models have two ear-shape handles, while others have a long wooden handle, sometimes combined with a short opposite handle that makes it easy to lift the pan. The most useful woks are made from heavy carbon steel, which distributes the heat quickly and evenly. Stainless steel woks tend to scorch and many nonstick woks cannot withstand the high temperature required for stir-frying. A new wok usually needs to be seasoned with oil and heat to create a natural nonstick patina. Follow the manufacturer's instructions. A wok with a diameter of 14 inches/35 cm is ideal for most family meals and one with a lid is more versatile.

> **Pans:** It is worth buying a selection of different-size pans with thick, flat bottoms and tight-fitting lids. It is also sensible to choose handles, including those on lids, that are heatproof and, if you are left-handed, to make sure that you can pour liquids and sauces safely and easily. The size of the pan directly affects the efficiency of the cooking. If it is too small, it is difficult to stir a dish and liquids can boil over. Some ingredients may be cooked through while others are still almost raw. If the pan is too large, again the cooking may not be even and will take longer—you are also wasting heat. Nonstick linings are a matter of personal choice.

Skillet: A large (9–11-inch/23–28-cm) heavy skillet with gently sloping sides is invaluable for softening onions, browning meat, and so on. If it has a heatproof handle, it can also be used under the broiler or even in the oven. A smaller skillet is ideal for dry-frying spices, seeds, and nuts and for cooking omelets. Nonstick pans produce healthier meals because they reduce the amount of oil required, and they are very easy to clean.

> **Grill pan:** This may be either flat or ridged and is usually made of cast iron for even distribution of heat. It is designed to be used over high, fast-cooking heat. Ridged pans prevent the ingredients from soaking in oil or fat, and will give the food you're cooking those characteristic charred lines.

> **Steamer:** Steaming is an economical and healthy way of cooking with the food placed in a perforated container over a boiling liquid—water, stock, or wine. The simplest way to do this is to stand a heatproof bowl on top of a grooved trivet in the bottom of a pan partly filled with simmering water. A tiered, stacking steel steamer is more versatile, letting you stew a dish in the bottom container while steaming vegetables above. A fold-out, tulip-shape steamer, available in two sizes, fits almost any size of pan but its central stalk slightly limits the quantity of ingredients you can steam. A universal steamer has a round, firm, perforated, stepped bottom that will fit on top of any pan. It is an extremely useful utensil. Stacking bamboo steamers with lids are usually used in a wok. Soak them well in cold water before using for the first time. If you find that you like the taste of steamed food, you may want to invest in an electronic food steamer. These have separate tiers or compartments for cooking different foods, and can be fully dismantled for easy cleaning.

> **Knives:** Good-quality, heavy knives are essential in any kitchen—cook's, utility, paring, and vegetable knives are the minimum requirement. Before buying, check that the weight of the knife is evenly balanced and that the handle feels comfortable. Store them in a knife block and keep them well sharpened with a V-sharpener, carborundum stone, or steel. Sharp knives are more efficient and are safer because they are less likely to slip.

> **Vegetable peeler:** The all-metal, swivel-blade peeler is the best known type and it is very easy to use. It peels thinly and is suitable for both left- and right-handed cooks. The Y-shape peeler also has a swivel blade and a sturdy handle that is easy to grasp. Besides peeling fruit and vegetables, these inexpensive tools are good for destringing celery and rhubarb, and shaving chocolate and hard cheeses, such as Parmesan.

> **Handheld mixer:** A mixer with rotary beaters takes the hard work out of mixing together ingredients. A smaller version known as a stick mixer is useful for blending soups and sauces while still in the pan.

> **Food processor:** An expensive piece of equipment that is bulky enough to cause storage problems in a small kitchen, nevertheless, this can be a great time-saver and take the hard work out of many jobs in the kitchen. Besides reducing mixtures to a puree, it can be used for chopping, slicing, grinding, beating, whisking, and making breadcrumbs. For durability, choose a model with a powerful motor.

meat

>4

>5

>6

grilled steak with hot chile salsa

serves 4

ingredients
sunflower oil, for brushing
4 sirloin steaks, about 8 oz/
  225 g each
salt and pepper

hot chile salsa
4 fresh red habanero chiles
4 fresh green poblano chiles
3 tomatoes, peeled, seeded,
  and diced
2 tbsp chopped fresh cilantro

1 tbsp red wine vinegar
2 tbsp olive oil
salt

corn salad or arugula,
  to garnish

>1 For the salsa, preheat the broiler to high. Arrange the chiles on a foil-lined broiler rack and cook under the preheated broiler, turning frequently, until blackened and charred.

>2 Let cool. When cool enough to handle, peel off the skins.

>3 Halve and seed the chiles, then finely chop the flesh.

>4 Mix together the chiles, tomatoes, and cilantro in a bowl.

>5 Mix together the vinegar and olive oil in a pitcher. Season to taste with salt and pour over the salsa. Toss well, cover, and chill until required.

>6 Heat a ridged grill pan over medium heat and brush lightly with sunflower oil. Season the steaks to taste with salt and pepper, and cook for 2–4 minutes on each side, or until cooked to your liking.

Serve immediately with the salsa, garnished
with corn salad.

teriyaki steak

serves 4

ingredients

4 beef steaks, about 5½ oz/
  150 g each
2 tbsp vegetable oil
generous 1¼ cups fresh bean
  sprouts

4 scallions, trimmed and finely
  sliced
salt and pepper

teriyaki sauce

2 tbsp mirin (Japanese
  rice wine)
2 tbsp sake or pale dry sherry
4 tbsp dark soy sauce

1 tsp granulated or superfine
  sugar

>1 Season the steaks to taste with salt and pepper and set aside.

>2 For the sauce, combine the mirin, sake, soy sauce, and sugar in a bowl, stirring well.

>3 Heat 1 tablespoon of oil in a skillet over high heat. Add the bean sprouts and fry quickly, tossing in the hot oil for 30 seconds.

>4 Remove from the skillet and drain on paper towels.

>5 Add the remaining oil to the skillet and, when hot, add the steaks. Cook for 1–3 minutes on each side, or until cooked to your liking. Remove from the skillet and keep warm.

>6 Remove the skillet from the heat and add the sauce and scallions. Return to the heat and simmer for 2 minutes, stirring, until the sauce thickens slightly and is glossy.

Slice each steak and arrange on a bed of bean sprouts. Spoon over the sauce and serve immediately.

paprika steak wraps with horseradish cream

serves 4

ingredients

4 sirloin steaks, about 6 oz/
  175 g each
1 garlic clove, crushed
2 tsp smoked paprika, plus
  extra for sprinkling
sunflower oil, for brushing
scant ½ cup sour cream
3 tbsp creamed horseradish
8 small flour tortillas
⅓ cup arugula leaves
2 firm, ripe avocados, peeled,
  pitted, and sliced
1 red onion, thinly sliced
salt and pepper

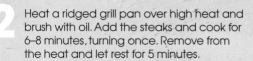

>1 Spread the steaks with garlic and sprinkle both sides with the paprika. Season to taste with salt and pepper.

>2 Heat a ridged grill pan over high heat and brush with oil. Add the steaks and cook for 6–8 minutes, turning once. Remove from the heat and let rest for 5 minutes.

Serve the wraps with a spoonful of horseradish cream, sprinkled with extra paprika.

>3 Mix together the sour cream and horseradish, then spread half over the tortillas.

>4 Slice the steaks into strips. Divide among the tortillas with the arugula, avocado, and onion, wrapping the sides over.

hot sesame beef

serves 4

ingredients

1 lb 2 oz/500 g beef tenderloin,
  cut into thin strips
1½ tbsp sesame seeds
½ cup beef stock
2 tbsp soy sauce

2 tbsp grated fresh ginger
2 garlic cloves, finely chopped
1 tsp cornstarch
½ tsp chile flakes
3 tbsp sesame oil

1 large head broccoli,
  cut into florets
1 yellow bell pepper, seeded
  and thinly sliced
1 fresh red chile, finely sliced
1 tbsp chili oil, to taste

salt and pepper
cooked wild rice, to serve
1 tbsp chopped fresh cilantro,
  to garnish

> **1** Mix the beef strips with 1 tablespoon of the sesame seeds in a small bowl.

> **2** In a separate bowl, stir together the stock, soy sauce, ginger, garlic, cornstarch, and chile flakes.

> **3** Heat 1 tablespoon of the sesame oil in a wok. Stir-fry the beef for 2–3 minutes. Remove and set aside, then wipe the wok clean with paper towels.

> **4** Heat the remaining sesame oil in the wok, add the broccoli, bell pepper, chile, and chili oil and stir-fry for 2–3 minutes.

>5 Stir in the stock mixture, cover, and simmer for 2 minutes.

>6 Return the beef to the wok and simmer until the juices thicken, stirring occasionally. Cook for an additional 1–2 minutes. Sprinkle with the remaining sesame seeds and season to taste with salt and pepper.

Serve over wild rice and garnish with cilantro.

chorizo, chile & chickpea casserole

serves 4

ingredients

2 tbsp olive oil
1 onion, sliced
1 large yellow bell pepper,
  seeded and sliced

1 garlic clove, crushed
1 tsp chile flakes
8 oz/225 g chorizo sausage
14 oz/400 g canned chopped
  tomatoes

14 oz/400 g canned chickpeas,
  drained
1 cup basmati rice
handful of arugula leaves
salt and pepper

4 tbsp coarsely chopped fresh
  basil, to garnish

>1 Heat the oil in a flameproof casserole and fry the onion over medium heat, stirring occasionally, for 5 minutes.

>2 Add the bell pepper, garlic, and chile flakes and cook for 2 minutes, stirring.

>3 Chop the chorizo into bite-size chunks and stir into the casserole.

>4 Add the tomatoes and chickpeas with salt and pepper to taste. Bring to a boil, cover, and simmer for 10 minutes.

>5 Meanwhile, cook the rice in a saucepan of lightly salted boiling water for 10–12 minutes, until tender. Drain.

>6 Stir in the arugula into the casserole.

Serve spooned over the rice, garnished with basil.

pork & rosemary burgers

serves 4

ingredients
1 lb 2 oz/500 g ground pork
1 small onion, finely chopped
1 garlic clove, crushed
1 tbsp finely chopped fresh
  rosemary
oil, for brushing
1 small baguette,
  split and cut into four
2 tomatoes, sliced
4 dill pickles, sliced
4 tbsp strained plain yogurt
2 tbsp chopped fresh mint
salt and pepper

> **1** Use your hands to mix together the pork, onion, garlic, and rosemary with salt and pepper to taste.

> **2** Divide into four and shape into flat burger shapes.

Spoon the minty yogurt over the burgers and replace the baguette tops to serve.

>3 Brush a ridged grill pan or skillet with oil and cook the burgers for 6–8 minutes, turning once, until golden and cooked through.

>4 Place a burger on the bottom half of each piece of baguette and top with the tomatoes and dill pickles. Mix together the yogurt and mint.

pork in plum sauce

serves 4

ingredients

1 lb 5 oz/600 g pork tenderloin
2 tbsp peanut oil
1 orange bell pepper, seeded
 and sliced

1 bunch of scallions, sliced
3⅔ cups sliced oyster
 mushrooms
5¼ cups fresh bean sprouts
2 tbsp dry sherry

⅔ cup plum sauce
9 oz/250 g medium egg
 noodles
salt and pepper
chopped fresh cilantro,
 to garnish

>**1** Slice the pork into long, thin strips.

>**2** Heat the oil in a wok and stir-fry the pork for 2–3 minutes.

>**3** Add the bell pepper and stir-fry for 2 minutes, then add the scallions, mushrooms, and bean sprouts.

>**4** Stir-fry for 2–3 minutes, then add the sherry and plum sauce and heat until boiling. Season well with salt and pepper.

>5 Cook the noodles in a saucepan of lightly salted boiling water for 4 minutes or according to the package directions, until tender.

>6 Drain the noodles, then add to the wok and toss well.

Serve immediately, garnished with cilantro.

turkey steaks with prosciutto & sage

serves 2

ingredients
2 skinless, boneless turkey steaks
2 slices prosciutto, halved

4 fresh sage leaves
2 tbsp all-purpose flour
2 tbsp olive oil

1 tbsp butter
salt and pepper
lemon wedges, to serve

> 1 Slice each turkey steak in half horizontally into 2 thinner scallops.

> 2 Put each scallop between 2 sheets of plastic wrap and pat out thinly with a rolling pin. Season each scallop with salt and pepper to taste.

Lay a half slice of prosciutto on each scallop, put a sage leaf on top, and secure with a toothpick.

> 4 Mix the flour with salt and pepper to taste on a large plate. Dust both sides of each scallop with the seasoned flour.

> **5** Heat the oil in a large skillet, add the butter, and heat until foaming. Add the scallops and fry over high heat for 1½ minutes, sage-side down.

> **6** Turn the scallops over and fry for an additional 30 seconds, until golden brown and cooked through.

Serve immediately with lemon wedges for squeezing over.

creamy turkey & broccoli gnocchi

serves 4

ingredients

1 tbsp sunflower oil
1 lb 2 oz/500 g turkey, cut into
  strips
2 small leeks, sliced diagonally
1 lb 2 oz/500 g store-bought
  fresh gnocchi
1 head broccoli, cut into
  bite-size pieces
⅓ cup sour cream
1 tbsp whole grain mustard
3 tbsp orange juice
salt and pepper
3 tbsp toasted pine nuts,
  to serve

> **1** Heat the oil in a wok or large skillet, then add the turkey and leeks and stir-fry over high heat for 5–6 minutes.

> **2** Meanwhile, bring a saucepan of lightly salted water to a boil. Add the gnocchi and broccoli, then cook for 3–4 minutes.

Serve immediately, sprinkled with
pine nuts.

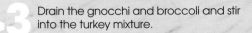>3 Drain the gnocchi and broccoli and stir
into the turkey mixture.

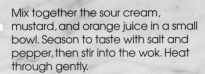>4 Mix together the sour cream,
mustard, and orange juice in a small
bowl. Season to taste with salt and
pepper, then stir into the wok. Heat
through gently.

baked tapenade chicken

serves 4

ingredients

4 skinless, boneless chicken
  breasts
4 tbsp green olive tapenade

8 thin slices smoked pancetta
2 garlic cloves, coarsely
  chopped

9 oz/250 g cherry tomatoes,
  halved
scant ½ cup dry white wine
2 tbsp olive oil

8 slices ciabatta
salt and pepper

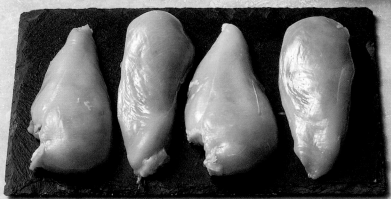

46

>**1** Preheat the oven to 425°F/220°C. Put the chicken breasts on a cutting board and cut three deep slashes into each.

>**2** Spread a tablespoon of the tapenade over each chicken breast, pushing it into the slashes with a palette knife.

>**3** Wrap each chicken breast in two slices of pancetta.

>**4** Place the chicken breasts in a shallow ovenproof dish and arrange the garlic and tomatoes around them.

>5 Season to taste with salt and pepper, then pour over the wine and 1 tablespoon of the oil.

>6 Bake in the preheated oven for about 20 minutes, until the juices run clear when the chicken is pierced with a skewer.

>7 Cover the dish loosely with aluminum foil and let stand for 5 minutes.

>8 Meanwhile, preheat the broiler to high. Brush the ciabatta with the remaining oil and cook under the preheated broiler for 2–3 minutes, turning once, until golden.

Transfer the chicken and tomatoes to serving plates and spoon over the juices. Serve with the toasted ciabatta.

steamed chicken with chile & cilantro butter

serves 4

ingredients

4 tbsp butter, softened
1 fresh Thai chile, seeded and
  chopped

3 tbsp chopped fresh cilantro
4 skinless, boneless
  chicken breasts, about
  6 oz/175 g each

1¾ cups coconut milk
1½ cups chicken stock
1 cup basmati rice
salt and pepper

pickled vegetables

1 carrot
½ cucumber
3 scallions
2 tbsp rice vinegar

50

1 Mix the butter with the chile and cilantro.

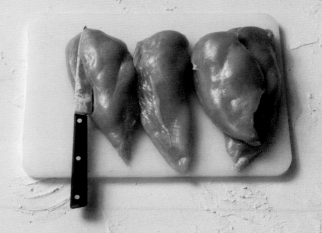 **2** Cut a deep slash into the side of each chicken breast to form a pocket.

3 Spoon quarter of the flavoured butter into each pocket and place on a 12-inch/30-cm square of baking parchment.

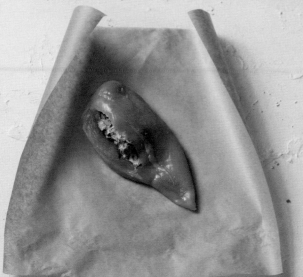

4 Season to taste with salt and pepper, then bring together 2 opposite sides of the paper on top, folding over to seal firmly. Twist the ends to seal.

>5 Pour the coconut milk and stock into a large pan with a steamer top. Bring to a boil. Stir in the rice with a pinch of salt.

>6 Put the chicken parcels in the steamer top, cover, and simmer for 15–18 minutes, stirring the rice once, until the rice is tender and the chicken is cooked through.

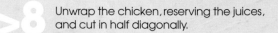

>7 Meanwhile, peel the carrot, then trim the carrot, cucumber, and scallions and cut into fine sticks. Sprinkle with the vinegar.

>8 Unwrap the chicken, reserving the juices, and cut in half diagonally.

Serve the chicken on the rice, with the juices spooned over and pickled vegetables on the side.

chicken with creamy penne

serves 2

ingredients
7 oz/200 g dried penne
1 tbsp olive oil
2 skinless, boneless chicken
 breasts
4 tbsp dry white wine
generous 1 cup frozen peas
5 tbsp heavy cream
salt
4–5 tbsp chopped fresh parsley,
 to garnish

>1 Bring a large saucepan of lightly salted water to a boil. Add the penne and cook for about 8–10 minutes, until tender but still firm to the bite.

>2 Meanwhile, heat the oil in a skillet, add the chicken, and cook over medium heat for about 4 minutes on each side.

Garnish with parsley and serve.

>3 Pour in the wine and cook over high heat until it has almost evaporated.

>4 Drain the pasta. Add the peas, cream, and pasta to the skillet and stir well. Cover and simmer for 2 minutes.

duck breasts with citrus glaze

serves 4

ingredients

¼ cup light brown sugar,
  plus extra if needed
finely grated rind and juice of
  1 orange

finely grated rind and juice of
  1 large lemon
finely grated rind and juice of
  1 lime
4 duck breasts, skin on

2 tbsp olive oil
salt and pepper
freshly cooked sugar snap
  peas and orange wedges,
  to serve

>1 Put the sugar in a small saucepan, add just enough water to cover, and heat gently until dissolved.

>2 Add the citrus rinds and juices and bring to a boil.

>3 Reduce the heat and simmer for about 10 minutes, until syrupy. Remove from the heat. Taste and add extra sugar if needed. Keep warm.

>4 Meanwhile, score the skin of the duck breasts with a sharp knife in a crisscross pattern and rub with salt and pepper.

>5 Heat the oil in a skillet. Place the duck breasts skin-side down in the skillet and cook for 5 minutes on each side, until the flesh is just pink. Keep warm.

>6 Slice the duck breasts diagonally into 5–6 slices and transfer to warmed plates.

Arrange some sugar snap peas and orange wedges on each plate, spoon over the glaze, and serve immediately.

honeyed apricot lamb with lemon couscous

serves 4

ingredients

4 lamb leg steaks
4 tsp ground coriander
1 tbsp ground cumin
1 small butternut squash
1 tbsp olive oil

1 onion, chopped
2½ cups chicken stock
2 tbsp chopped fresh ginger
scant ½ cup plumped dried
  apricots
2 tbsp honey

finely grated rind and juice of
  1 lemon
generous 1 cup couscous
salt and pepper
3 tbsp chopped fresh mint,
  to garnish

>1
Sprinkle the lamb steaks with the coriander and cumin.

>2
Peel and seed the squash and cut into bite-size chunks.

>3
Heat the oil in a flameproof casserole. Add the lamb and cook over high heat for 2–3 minutes, turning once.

>4
Stir in the squash, onion, and half the stock, then bring to a boil.

> **5** Add the ginger, apricots, honey, and lemon juice. Season to taste with salt and pepper. Cover and cook over medium heat for about 20 minutes, stirring occasionally.

> **6** Meanwhile, bring the remaining stock to a boil in a small saucepan, then stir in the couscous and lemon rind with salt and pepper to taste. Remove from the heat, cover, and let stand for 5 minutes.

Serve the lamb with the couscous,
garnished with mint.

orange & lemon crispy lamb chops

serves 2

ingredients
1 garlic clove, crushed
1 tbsp olive oil
2 tbsp finely grated orange rind
2 tbsp finely grated lemon rind
6 lamb chops
salt and pepper
orange wedges, to garnish

> **>1** Preheat a ridged grill pan.

> **>2** Mix together the garlic, oil, and citrus rinds in a bowl. Season to taste with salt and pepper.

Garnish with the orange wedges and serve.

>3 Brush the mixture over the lamb chops.

>4 Cook the chops in the preheated grill pan for 4–5 minutes on each side.

>1

>2

>3

fish

>4

>5

>6

seared sesame salmon with bok choy

serves 4

ingredients

1-inch/2.5-cm piece fresh
  ginger
1 tbsp soy sauce

1 tsp sesame oil
4 skinless salmon fillets
2 tbsp sesame seeds
lime wedges, to serve

stir-fry
2 small bok choy
1 bunch of scallions
1 tbsp sunflower oil

1 tsp sesame oil
salt and pepper

> **1** Peel and finely grate the ginger, then combine with the soy sauce and sesame oil in a shallow dish that is large enough to hold the salmon fillets in a single layer.

> **2** Add the salmon fillets, turning to coat evenly on both sides.

> **3** Sprinkle one side of the salmon with half the sesame seeds, then turn and sprinkle the other side with the remaining sesame seeds.

> **4** Cut the bok choy lengthwise into quarters.

>5 Cut the scallions into thick diagonal slices.

>6 Preheat a heavy-bottom skillet. Add the salmon and cook for 3–4 minutes. Turn and cook for an additional 3–4 minutes.

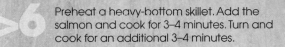

>7 Meanwhile, heat the sunflower and sesame oils in a wok, add the bok choy and scallions, and stir-fry for 2–3 minutes. Season to taste with salt and pepper.

>8 Divide the vegetables among warmed serving plates and put the salmon on top.

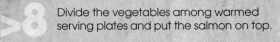

Serve immediately with lime wedges for
squeezing over.

fish goujons with chili mayonnaise

serves 4

ingredients

scant 1½ cups all-purpose flour
3 eggs
generous 1 cup matzo meal

1 lb/450 g firm whitefish fillets,
  cut into strips
sunflower oil or peanut oil,
  for shallow-frying
salt and pepper

chili mayonnaise

2 tbsp sweet chili sauce
4–5 tbsp mayonnaise

> **1** Mix the flour with plenty of salt and pepper on a large flat plate.

> **2** Beat the eggs in a bowl.

> **3** Spread out the matzo meal on another flat plate.

> **4** Dip the fish pieces into the seasoned flour, then into the beaten egg and finally into the matzo meal, ensuring a generous coating.

> **5** Heat ½ inch/1 cm of oil in a nonstick skillet. Cook the fish pieces in batches for a few minutes, turning once, until golden and cooked through.

> **6** For the chili mayonnaise, put the chili sauce and mayonnaise in a bowl and beat together until combined.

Transfer the fish to warmed plates and
serve with the chili mayonnaise on the side.

peppered
tuna steaks

serves 4

ingredients

4 tuna steaks, about 6 oz/
175 g each
4 tsp sunflower oil or olive oil
1 tsp salt
2 tbsp pink, green, and black
peppercorns, coarsely
crushed
handful of fresh arugula leaves,
to garnish
lemon wedges, to serve

>1 Brush the tuna steaks with the oil.

>2 Sprinkle with the salt.

Garsish with arugula and serve with the lemon wedges for squeezing over.

>3 Coat the tuna with the crushed peppercorns.

>4 Meanwhile, heat a ridged grill pan over medium heat. Add the tuna and cook for 2–3 minutes on each side.

quick & creamy fish pie

serves 4

ingredients

1 tbsp olive oil
2 shallots, finely chopped
⅔ cup dry white wine
1 bay leaf

generous 2¾ cups thickly sliced
  mushrooms
scant ½ cup sour cream
1 lb 2 oz/500 g firm whitefish
  fillets, cut into chunks

6 oz/175 g cooked, peeled
  shrimp
1½ cups frozen peas
3 tbsp melted butter
2¾ cups fresh white
  breadcrumbs

salt and pepper
chopped fresh parsley,
  to garnish

>1 Preheat the broiler to medium. Heat the oil in an ovenproof saucepan or a shallow flameproof casserole and fry the shallots for 2–3 minutes, until softened.

>2 Add the wine, bay leaf, and mushrooms and simmer for 2 minutes, stirring occasionally.

>3 Stir in the sour cream and add the fish. Season to taste with salt and pepper.

>4 Bring to a boil, cover, and simmer for 5–6 minutes, until the fish is almost cooked.

>5 Remove and discard the bay leaf, add the shrimp and peas, and return to a boil.

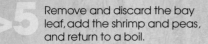

>6 Meanwhile, remelt the butter, if necessary, in a separate saucepan and stir in the breadcrumbs.

>7 Spread the breadcrumb mixture evenly over the top of the fish mixture.

>8 Put the saucepan under the preheated broiler for 3–4 minutes, until the topping is golden brown and bubbling.

Sprinkle with parsley and serve hot.

sea bass with olive gremolata

serves 4

ingredients
2 lb/900 g small new potatoes
4 sea bass fillets, about 6 oz/
   175 g each
1 tbsp olive oil

4 tbsp dry white wine
salt and pepper

olive gremolata
grated rind of 1 lemon
1 garlic clove, chopped
2 large handfuls of fresh
   flat-leaf parsley (about 1 cup)

⅔ cup pitted black olives
2 tbsp capers
2 tbsp olive oil

> **1** Cook the potatoes in a saucepan of lightly salted boiling water for 15–20 minutes, or until tender.

> **2** Meanwhile, make the gremolata. Put the lemon rind, garlic, parsley, olives, capers, and oil in a food processor and process briefly to form a coarse paste.

> **3** Brush the sea bass with the oil and season to taste with salt and pepper. Heat a heavy skillet and fry the sea bass for 5–6 minutes, turning once.

> **4** Remove the fish from the skillet and keep warm. Stir the wine into the skillet and boil for 1 minute, stirring.

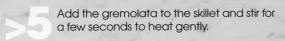

>5 Add the gremolata to the skillet and stir for a few seconds to heat gently.

>6 Drain the potatoes when tender and crush lightly with a wooden spoon or potato masher.

Serve the sea bass and crushed potatoes topped with the gremolata.

speedy tuna pizza

serves 4

ingredients

3 tbsp red pesto
1 x 12-inch/30-cm
  store-bought pizza crust
7 oz/200 g canned tuna in
  sunflower oil, drained
6 oz/175 g cherry plum
  tomatoes, halved
scant 1 cup diced
  mozzarella cheese
2 tbsp capers
8 small pitted black olives
1 tbsp olive oil
salt and pepper

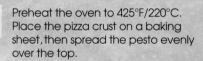

>1 Preheat the oven to 425°F/220°C. Place the pizza crust on a baking sheet, then spread the pesto evenly over the top.

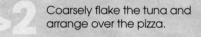

>2 Coarsely flake the tuna and arrange over the pizza.

Serve the pizza hot or cold.

>3 Scatter over the tomatoes, mozzarella, capers, and olives. Season to taste with salt and pepper.

>4 Drizzle the oil over the pizza and bake in the preheated oven for about 15 minutes, or until golden and bubbling.

hot-smoked salmon on hash browns

serves 4

ingredients

1 onion
1 lb 2 oz/800 g starchy
  potatoes, peeled

2 tbsp chopped fresh dill,
  plus extra sprigs to garnish
1 tsp celery salt
2 tbsp butter

2 tbsp olive oil
1 bunch watercress
1 tbsp walnut oil
2 tbsp lemon juice

9 oz/250 g hot-smoked salmon,
  coarsely flaked
pepper
lemon wedges, to serve

>1 Peel the onion, then grate the onion and potatoes in a food processor. Tip into a clean dish towel and squeeze out as much moisture as possible.

>2 Stir in the chopped dill and celery salt and season well with pepper. Divide into 8 portions.

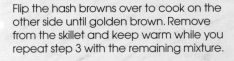

>3 Melt half the butter and half the olive oil in a large skillet. Add 4 heaps of the potato mixture and flatten lightly. Fry for 4–5 minutes, until golden underneath.

>4 Flip the hash browns over to cook on the other side until golden brown. Remove from the skillet and keep warm while you repeat step 3 with the remaining mixture.

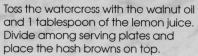

>5 Toss the watercress with the walnut oil and 1 tablespoon of the lemon juice. Divide among serving plates and place the hash browns on top.

>6 Top with the salmon and sprinkle with the remaining lemon juice and pepper to taste.

Garnish with dill sprigs and serve
with lemon wedges.

spicy thai seafood stew

serves 4

ingredients

7 oz/200 g squid, cleaned and tentacles discarded

1 lb 2 oz/500 g firm whitefish fillets

1 tbsp corn oil

4 shallots, finely chopped

2 garlic cloves, finely chopped

2 tbsp Thai green curry paste

2 small lemongrass stalks, finely chopped

1 tsp shrimp paste

generous 2 cups coconut milk

7 oz/200 g jumbo shrimp, peeled and deveined

12 clams, scrubbed

8 fresh basil leaves, finely shredded, plus extra leaves to garnish

freshly cooked rice, to serve

>1 Using a sharp knife, cut the squid into thick rings and cut the fish into bite-size chunks.

>2 Preheat a large wok, then add the oil and heat. Add the shallots, garlic, and curry paste and stir-fry for 1–2 minutes.

>3 Add the lemongrass and shrimp paste, then stir in the coconut milk and bring to a boil.

>4 Reduce the heat until the liquid is simmering gently, then add the squid, fish, and shrimp and simmer for 2 minutes.

Discard any clams with broken shells and any that refuse to close when tapped. Add the clams to the wok and simmer for an additional minute, or until the clams have opened. Discard any that remain closed.

>6 Sprinkle the shredded basil leaves over the stew.

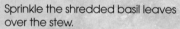

Transfer to serving plates, garnish with basil leaves, and serve immediately with freshly cooked rice.

spiced mackerel with tropical salsa

serves 4

ingredients
2 tsp ground coriander
2 tsp ground cumin
½ tsp ground turmeric
¼ tsp cayenne pepper
pinch of salt
8 mackerel fillets
flatbreads, to serve

salsa
1 small avocado
1 small mango
1 small onion, finely chopped
juice of 1 lime

>1 Preheat a ridged grill pan until hot. Mix together the coriander, cumin, turmeric, cayenne, and salt.

>2 Cut deep slashes in the skin side of each mackerel fillet and rub the spices all over.

Serve the mackerel with the salsa spooned over, accompanied by flatbreads.

>3 For the salsa, halve, pit, and peel the avocado and mango, then cut into fine dice. Mix with the onion and lime juice.

>4 Cook the mackerel in the preheated grill pan for 6–8 minutes, turning once, until cooked through.

linguine with sardines

serves 4

ingredients

8 sardines, filleted, washed, and
  dried
4 tbsp olive oil

3 garlic cloves, sliced
1 tsp chile flakes
1 fennel bulb, trimmed and
  thinly sliced

12 oz/350 g dried linguine
½ tsp finely grated lemon rind
1 tbsp lemon juice
2 tbsp toasted pine nuts

2 tbsp chopped fresh parsley
salt and pepper

> **1** Chop the sardines into large pieces and reserve.

> **2** Heat 2 tablespoons of the oil in a large skillet over medium–high heat and add the garlic and chile flakes.

> **3** Cook for 1 minute, then add the fennel. Cook, stirring occasionally, for 4–5 minutes, or until softened.

> **4** Reduce the heat, add the sardine pieces, and cook for an additional 3–4 minutes.

> **5** Meanwhile, bring a large saucepan of lightly salted water to a boil. Add the pasta and cook for 8–10 minutes, or until tender but still firm to the bite.

> **6** Drain thoroughly and return to the pan.

> **7** Add the lemon rind, lemon juice, pine nuts, and parsley to the sardine mixture and toss together. Season to taste with salt and pepper.

> **8** Add to the pasta with the remaining oil and toss together gently.

Transfer to a warmed serving dish and serve immediately.

calamari with shrimp & fava beans

serves 4–6

ingredients

2 tbsp olive oil
4 scallions, thinly sliced
2 garlic cloves, finely chopped

1 lb 2 oz/500 g cleaned squid
  bodies, thickly sliced
⅓ cup dry white wine

1½ cups fresh or frozen baby
  fava beans
9 oz/250 g jumbo shrimp,
  shelled and deveined

4 tbsp chopped fresh flat-leaf
  parsley
salt and pepper
crusty bread, to serve

> **1** Heat the oil in a large skillet with a lid, add the scallions, and cook over medium heat, stirring occasionally, for 4–5 minutes, until softened.

> **2** Add the garlic and cook, stirring, for 30 seconds, until softened.

> **3** Add the squid and cook over high heat, stirring occasionally, for 2 minutes, or until golden brown.

> **4** Add the wine and bring to a boil. Add the beans, reduce the heat, cover, and simmer for 5–8 minutes, if using fresh beans, or 4–5 minutes, if using frozen beans, until tender.

>5
Add the shrimp, re-cover, and simmer for an additional 2–3 minutes, until the shrimp turn pink and start to curl.

>6
Stir in the parsley and season to taste with salt and pepper.

Serve hot with crusty bread to mop
up the juices.

monkfish with a lemon & parsley crust

serves 4

ingredients

4 tbsp sunflower oil
4 tbsp fresh breadcrumbs
4 tbsp chopped fresh parsley,
  plus extra sprigs to garnish
finely grated rind of 1 large
  lemon
4 monkfish fillets, about
  5–6 oz/140–175 g each
salt and pepper

> **1** Preheat the oven to 350°F/180°C. Mix together the oil, breadcrumbs, parsley, and lemon rind until well combined. Season to taste with salt and pepper.

> **2** Place the fish fillets in a large roasting pan.

Garnish with parsley sprigs and serve.

> 3

Divide the breadcrumb mixture among the fish and press it down with your fingers to ensure it covers the fillets.

> 4

Bake in the preheated oven for 7–8 minutes, or until the fish is cooked through.

thai shrimp noodle bowl

serves 4

ingredients

1 bunch of scallions
2 celery stalks
1 red bell pepper
7 oz/200 g rice vermicelli
  noodles

2 tbsp peanut oil
½ cup unsalted peanuts
1 fresh Thai chile, sliced
1 lemongrass stalk, crushed
1¾ cups fish or chicken stock
scant 1 cup coconut milk

2 tsp Thai fish sauce
12 oz/350 g cooked, peeled
  jumbo shrimp
salt and pepper
3 tbsp chopped fresh cilantro,
  to garnish

>1 Trim the scallions and celery and thinly slice diagonally. Seed and thinly slice the bell pepper.

>2 Put the noodles into a bowl, cover with boiling water, and let stand for 4 minutes or according to the package directions, until tender. Drain.

>3 Heat the oil in a wok and stir-fry the peanuts for 1–2 minutes, until golden. Lift out with a slotted spoon.

>4 Add the sliced scallions, celery, and bell pepper to the wok and stir-fry over high heat for 1–2 minutes.

>5 Add the chile, lemongrass, stock, coconut milk, and fish sauce and bring to a boil.

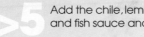

>6 Stir in the shrimp, then return to a boil, stirring. Season to taste with salt and pepper, then add the noodles.

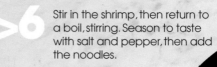

Serve in warmed bowls, sprinkled
with cilantro.

ginger shrimp with oyster mushrooms

serves 4

ingredients

⅔ cup chicken stock
2 tsp sesame seeds
3 tsp grated fresh ginger
1 tbsp soy sauce
¼ tsp hot pepper sauce

1 tsp cornstarch
3 tbsp vegetable oil
3 carrots, peeled and thinly
  sliced
7 cups thinly sliced oyster
  mushrooms

1 large red bell pepper, seeded
  and thinly sliced
1 lb/450 g large shrimp, peeled
  and deveined
2 garlic cloves, crushed

freshly cooked rice, to serve
fresh cilantro sprigs, to garnish

>**1** In a small bowl, stir together the stock, sesame seeds, ginger, soy sauce, hot pepper sauce, and cornstarch until well blended. Set aside.

>**2** Add 2 tablespoons of the oil to a large wok with a lid and heat. Stir-fry the carrots for 3 minutes, then remove from the wok and set aside.

>**3** Add the remaining oil to the wok and stir-fry the mushrooms for 2 minutes. Remove from the wok and set aside.

>**4** Add the bell pepper, shrimp, and garlic to the wok and stir-fry for 3 minutes, until the shrimp turn pink and start to curl.

>5 Stir the stock mixture, then pour it into the wok.

>6 Cook until the mixture bubbles, then return the carrots and mushrooms to the wok. Cover and cook for an additional 2 minutes, until heated through.

Serve over freshly cooked rice and garnish with cilantro sprigs.

wine-steamed mussels

serves 4

ingredients
8 tbsp butter
1 shallot, chopped
3 garlic cloves, finely chopped
4 lb 8 oz/2 kg mussels, scrubbed
  and debearded
1 cup dry white wine
½ tsp salt
4 tbsp chopped fresh parsley
pepper
fresh crusty bread, to serve

> **1** Place half the butter in a large saucepan and melt over low heat. Add the shallot and garlic and cook for 2 minutes.

> **2** Discard any mussels with broken shells and any that refuse to close when tapped. Add the mussels and wine to the pan with the salt and pepper to taste. Cover and bring to a boil, then cook for 3 minutes, shaking the pan from time to time.

Serve immediately with fresh crusty bread for mopping up the juices.

>3 Remove the mussels from the pan with a slotted spoon and place in individual serving bowls. Discard any mussels that remain closed.

>4 Stir the remaining butter and the parsley into the cooking juices in the pan. Bring to a boil, then pour over the mussels.

> 1

> 2

> 3

vegetarian

>4

>5

>6

risotto with asparagus & walnuts

serves 4

ingredients

1 tbsp butter
3 tbsp olive oil
1 small onion, finely chopped
scant 1¾ cups risotto rice

⅔ cup dry white wine
6¾ cups hot vegetable stock
7 oz/200 g asparagus stalks, cut
  into 2½-inch/6-cm lengths
⅓ cup chopped walnuts

grated rind of 1 lemon
salt and pepper
walnut oil, to serve (optional)
strips of lemon zest, to garnish

>1 Heat the butter and olive oil in a large saucepan and fry the onion, stirring, for 3–4 minutes, until softened.

>2 Add the rice and stir over medium heat for 1 minute, without browning.

>3 Add the wine and boil rapidly, stirring, until almost all evaporated.

>4 Stir the stock into the pan a ladleful at a time, letting each addition be absorbed before adding more.

>5 After 10 minutes, add the asparagus and continue cooking, adding stock when necessary.

>6 After an additional 5 minutes, test a grain of rice—it should be "al dente" or firm to the bite.

>7 Stir in the walnuts and lemon rind, then adjust the seasoning, adding salt and pepper to taste.

>8 Remove from the heat and drizzle over a little walnut oil, if using, stirring in lightly.

Serve the risotto immediately, garnished
with strips of lemon zest.

egg tortilla with feta & corn

serves 2

ingredients

12 oz/350 g potatoes
2 tbsp olive oil
1 onion, chopped

1 zucchini, coarsely grated
7 oz/200 g canned corn, drained
6 eggs

scant 1 cup crumbled feta cheese
salt and pepper
paprika, to garnish

>1 Preheat the broiler to high. Peel or scrub the potatoes and cut into ½-inch/1-cm dice.

>2 Cook the potatoes in a saucepan of lightly salted boiling water for 5 minutes, or until just tender. Drain.

>3 Heat the oil in a large ovenproof skillet over medium heat and fry the onion for about 5 minutes, until softened.

>4 Stir in the zucchini and potatoes, then cook for 2 minutes. Stir in the corn.

Beat the eggs lightly with salt and pepper to taste.

Stir the beaten eggs into the skillet, then scatter over the feta cheese. Cook for 4–6 minutes, until almost set.

Put the tortilla under the preheated broiler for 2–3 minutes, until set and golden brown.

Sprinkle the tortilla with paprika and cut into 4–6 wedges.

Serve the tortilla hot or cold.

macaroni & cheese

serves 4

ingredients

8 oz/225 g dried macaroni
generous 1 cup ricotta cheese
1½ tbsp whole grain mustard
3 tbsp snipped fresh chives,
  plus extra to garnish
7 oz/200 g cherry tomatoes,
  halved
scant 1 cup chopped drained
  sun-dried tomatoes in oil
butter or oil, for greasing
scant 1 cup grated cheddar
  cheese
salt and pepper

> **1** Preheat the broiler to high. Bring a large saucepan of lightly salted water to a boil. Add the pasta and cook for 10–12 minutes, or until tender but still firm to the bite. Drain.

> **2** Mix together the ricotta, mustard, and chives with salt and pepper to taste. Stir in the macaroni, cherry tomatoes, and sun-dried tomatoes.

Serve the macaroni sprinkled
with extra chives.

>3 Grease a 7½-cup shallow ovenproof dish.
Spoon in the macaroni, spreading evenly.

>4 Sprinkle the cheddar cheese over the
macaroni mixture and cook under the
preheated broiler for 4–5 minutes, until
golden and bubbling.

mushroom & cauliflower cheese crumble

serves 4

ingredients
1 cauliflower, cut into florets
4 tbsp butter
1⅔ cups sliced mushrooms
salt and pepper

topping
1⅔ cups dry breadcrumbs
2 tbsp grated Parmesan
  cheese
1 tsp dried oregano

1 tsp dried parsley
2 tbsp butter

>1 Bring a large saucepan of lightly salted water to a boil. Add the cauliflower and cook for 3 minutes.

>2 Remove from the heat, drain well, and transfer to a shallow, ovenproof dish.

>3 Preheat the oven to 450°F/230°C. Melt the butter in a small skillet over medium heat. Add the mushrooms, stir, and cook gently for 3 minutes.

>4 Remove from the heat and spoon on top of the cauliflower. Season to taste with salt and pepper.

>5 Combine the breadcrumbs, Parmesan, and herbs in a small bowl, then sprinkle over the vegetables.

>6 Dice the butter and dot over the breadcrumb mixture. Bake in the preheated oven for 15 minutes, or until the topping is golden brown.

Serve from the baking dish.

jamaican rice & beans with tofu

serves 4

ingredients

9 oz/250 g firm tofu
2 tbsp chopped fresh thyme,
  plus extra sprigs to garnish

2 tbsp olive oil
1 onion, sliced
1 garlic clove, crushed
1 small fresh red chile, chopped

1¾ cups vegetable stock
1 cup basmati rice
4 tbsp coconut cream

14 oz/400 g canned red kidney
  beans, drained
salt and pepper

>1 Cut the tofu into bite-size cubes. Toss with half the chopped thyme and sprinkle with salt and pepper to taste.

>2 Heat 1 tablespoon of the oil in a skillet and fry the tofu, stirring occasionally, for 2 minutes. Remove and keep warm.

>3 Fry the onion in the remaining oil, stirring, for 3–4 minutes.

>4 Stir in the garlic, chile, and remaining chopped thyme, then add the stock and bring to a boil.

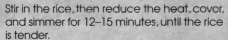 Stir in the rice, then reduce the heat, cover, and simmer for 12–15 minutes, until the rice is tender.

>6 Stir in the coconut cream and beans, season to taste with salt and pepper, and cook gently for 2–3 minutes.

Spoon the tofu over the rice and serve hot, garnished with thyme sprigs.

provolone cheese skewers on fennel & white bean salad

serves 4

ingredients
7 oz/200 g provolone cheese
1 garlic clove, crushed
1 fennel bulb, thinly sliced
1 small red onion, thinly sliced
14 oz/400 g canned cannellini
  beans, drained
balsamic vinegar, to serve

dressing
finely grated rind and juice
  of 1 lemon
3 tbsp chopped fresh flat-leaf
  parsley
4 tbsp olive oil
salt and pepper

> **1** Preheat the broiler to high. For the dressing, mix together the lemon rind and juice, parsley, and oil with salt and pepper to taste.

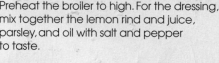

> **2** Cut the provolone into ¾-inch/2-cm cubes, thread onto 4 presoaked wooden skewers, and brush with the dressing.

Serve the skewers with the salad, sprinkled with a little balsamic vinegar.

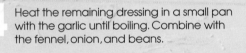 **>3** Cook the skewers under the preheated broiler for 6–8 minutes, turning once, until golden.

Heat the remaining dressing in a small pan with the garlic until boiling. Combine with the fennel, onion, and beans.

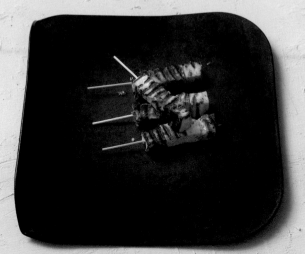

tofu stir-fry

serves 4

ingredients
2 tbsp sunflower oil
12 oz/350 g firm tofu, cubed

8 oz/225 g bok choy, coarsely
 chopped
1 garlic clove, chopped

4 tbsp sweet chili sauce
2 tbsp light soy sauce

>1 Heat 1 tablespoon of the oil in a wok.

>2 Add the tofu to the wok in batches and stir-fry for 2–3 minutes, until golden. Remove and set aside.

>3 Add the bok choy to the wok and stir-fry for a few seconds, until tender and wilted. Remove and set aside.

>4 Heat the remaining oil in the wok, then add the garlic and stir-fry for 30 seconds.

141

>5 Stir in the chili sauce and soy sauce and bring to a boil.

>6 Return the tofu and bok choy to the wok and toss gently until coated in the sauce.

Transfer to individual dishes and serve immediately.

fusilli with zucchini & lemon

serves 4

ingredients

6 tbsp olive oil
1 small onion, thinly sliced
2 garlic cloves, finely chopped
2 tbsp chopped fresh rosemary

1 tbsp chopped fresh flat-leaf
  parsley
1 lb/450 g small zucchini, cut
  into 1½-inch/4-cm strips
finely grated rind of 1 lemon

1 lb/450 g dried fusilli
salt and pepper
4 tbsp grated Parmesan
  cheese, to serve

>1 Heat the oil in a large skillet over low–medium heat. Add the onion and cook gently, stirring occasionally, for about 10 minutes, until golden.

>2 Increase the heat to medium–high. Add the garlic, rosemary, and parsley. Cook for a few seconds, stirring.

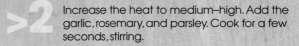

>3 Add the zucchini and lemon rind. Cook for 5–7 minutes, stirring occasionally, until just tender. Season to taste with salt and pepper. Remove from the heat.

>4 Bring a large saucepan of lightly salted water to a boil. Add the pasta, return to a boil, and cook for 8–10 minutes, or until tender but still firm to the bite.

>5 Drain the pasta and transfer to a warmed serving dish.

 >6 Briefly reheat the zucchini sauce. Pour over the pasta and toss well to mix.

Sprinkle with Parmesan cheese and serve immediately.

tomato ratatouille

serves 4

ingredients

1 tsp olive oil
1 onion, cut into small wedges
2–4 garlic cloves, chopped
1 small eggplant, chopped
1 red and 1 yellow bell pepper,
  seeded and chopped
1 zucchini, chopped
2 tbsp tomato paste
3 tbsp water
⅔ cup sliced mushrooms
2 ripe tomatoes, chopped
pepper
1 tbsp shredded fresh basil,
  to garnish
2 tbsp freshly grated Parmesan
  cheese, to serve

1 Heat the oil in a heavy saucepan. Add the onion, garlic, and eggplant and cook, stirring frequently, for 3 minutes.

2 Add the bell peppers and zucchini.

Divide the ratatouille among 4 warmed dishes, garnish with shredded basil, and serve with Parmesan cheese.

>3 Mix together the tomato paste and water in a small bowl and stir into the pan. Bring to a boil, cover, reduce the heat to a simmer, and cook for 10 minutes.

>4 Add the mushrooms and tomatoes, with pepper to taste, and continue to simmer for 12–15 minutes, stirring occasionally, until the vegetables are tender.

mushrooms & polenta with herb butter

serves 4

ingredients

9-oz/250-g block prepared
  polenta
4 large portobello mushrooms
5 tbsp butter

1 garlic clove, crushed
1 tbsp chopped fresh parsley
1 tbsp snipped fresh chives,
  plus extra to garnish
4 very fresh eggs

3½ oz/100 g baby spinach
  leaves
salt and pepper
fresh Parmesan cheese
  shavings, to serve

>1 Preheat the broiler to high. Cut the polenta into 8 slices and arrange on a foil-lined broiler rack with the mushrooms.

>2 Melt the butter in a small pan with the garlic. Stir in the parsley and chives.

>3 Brush the mushrooms and polenta with the herb butter and season to taste with salt and pepper.

>4 Cook under the preheated broiler for 6–8 minutes, turning once, until the polenta is golden and the mushrooms are tender.

>5 Bring a saucepan of water to just under boiling point. Break the eggs carefully into the water.

>6 Poach the eggs for about 3 minutes, until just set. Lift out with a slotted spoon.

>7 Put two slices of polenta on each serving plate and add a small handful of spinach leaves.

>8 Top each with a mushroom, then add a poached egg and spoon over the remaining herb butter.

Sprinkle with Parmesan shavings to serve and garnish with chives.

noodle stir-fry

serves 2

ingredients

5 oz/140 g flat rice noodles
6 tbsp soy sauce
2 tbsp lemon juice

1 tsp granulated sugar
½ tsp cornstarch
1 tbsp vegetable oil
2 tsp grated fresh ginger

2 garlic cloves, chopped
4–5 scallions, trimmed and
  sliced
2 tbsp rice wine or dry sherry

7 oz/200 g canned water
  chestnuts, drained and sliced

> **1** Put the noodles in a large bowl, cover with boiling water, and let stand for 4 minutes or according to the package directions, until tender. Drain and rinse under cold running water.

> **2** Mix together the soy sauce, lemon juice, sugar, and cornstarch in a small bowl. Set aside.

> **3** Heat the oil in a wok, add the ginger and garlic, and stir-fry for 1 minute.

> **4** Add the scallions and stir-fry for 3 minutes.

>5 Add the rice wine, then add the soy sauce mixture and cook for 1 minute.

>6 Stir in the water chestnuts and noodles and cook for an additional 1–2 minutes, or until heated through.

Transfer to individual dishes and serve immediately.

falafel
burgers

serves 4

ingredients
1 lb 12 oz/800 g canned
  chickpeas, drained
1 small onion, chopped
finely grated rind and juice
  of 1 lime
2 tsp ground coriander
2 tsp ground cumin
6 tbsp all-purpose flour
4 tbsp olive oil
salt and pepper
4 fresh basil sprigs, to garnish
tomato salsa, to serve

> **1** Put the chickpeas, onion, lime rind and
juice, and the spices into a food processor
and process to a coarse paste. Season
to taste with salt and pepper.

> **2** Tip the mixture out onto a clean
counter and shape into 4 patties.

Garnish with basil sprigs and serve with tomato salsa.

>3 Spread out the flour on a large flat plate and use to coat the patties.

>4 Heat the oil in a large skillet, add the patties, and cook for 2 minutes on each side, or until crisp.

tacos with chickpea salsa

serves 4

ingredients

2 firm, ripe avocados
1 tbsp lime juice
1 tomato, diced
1 tbsp olive oil

1 small onion, sliced
14 oz/400 g canned chickpeas,
  drained
1 tsp mild chili powder
8 romaine lettuce leaves

8 tacos
2 tbsp chopped fresh cilantro,
  plus extra sprigs to garnish
⅔ cup sour cream
salt and pepper

>1 Halve, pit, peel, and dice the avocados and toss with the lime juice.

>2 Stir in the tomato and season well with salt and pepper.

>3 Heat the oil in a saucepan and fry the onion for 3–4 minutes, or until golden brown.

>4 Mash the chickpeas with a fork and stir into the pan with the chili powder. Heat gently, stirring, for 2 minutes.

>5 Divide the lettuce among the tacos. Stir the chopped cilantro into the avocado-and-tomato mixture, then spoon into the tacos.

>6 Add a spoonful of the chickpea mixture to each taco and top with a spoonful of sour cream.

Garnish with cilantro sprigs and serve immediately.

goat cheese tarts

makes about 12

ingredients

melted butter, for greasing
14-oz/400-g package
 prepared and rolled puff
 pastry

all-purpose flour, for dusting
1 egg, beaten
about 3 tbsp onion relish or
 tomato relish

12 oz/350 g goat cheese logs,
 sliced into circles
olive oil, for drizzling
pepper

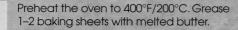

>1 Preheat the oven to 400°F/200°C. Grease 1–2 baking sheets with melted butter.

>2 Transfer the pastry sheet to a lightly floured counter and roll out lightly to remove any creases, if necessary.

>3 Use a 3-inch/7.5-cm pastry cutter to stamp out as many circles as possible.

>4 Place the circles on the prepared baking sheets and press gently about 1 inch/2.5 cm from the edge of each with a 2-inch/5-cm pastry cutter.

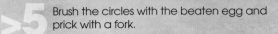

>5 Brush the circles with the beaten egg and prick with a fork.

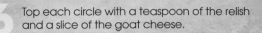

>6 Top each circle with a teaspoon of the relish and a slice of the goat cheese.

>7 Drizzle with oil and sprinkle over a little pepper.

>8 Bake in the preheated oven for 8–10 minutes, or until the pastry is crisp and the cheese is bubbling.

Serve warm.

zucchini, carrot & tomato frittata

serves 2–4

ingredients

1 tsp olive oil
1 onion, cut into
  small wedges
1–2 garlic cloves, crushed
2 eggs
2 egg whites
1 zucchini, grated
2 carrots, peeled and
  grated
2 tomatoes, chopped
pepper
1 tbsp shredded fresh basil,
  to garnish

>1 Heat the oil in a large nonstick skillet, add the onion and garlic, and sauté for 5 minutes, stirring frequently.

>2 Beat together the eggs and egg whites in a bowl, then pour into the skillet.

Sprinkle with the shredded basil, cut the frittata into quarters, and serve.

>3 Using a spatula, pull the egg mixture from the sides of the skillet into the center, letting the uncooked egg run underneath.

>4 When the bottom has set lightly, add the zucchini, carrots, and tomatoes. Season to taste with pepper and continue to cook over low heat until the eggs are cooked to your liking.

desserts

>4

>5

>6

quick tiramisù

serves 4

ingredients

1 cup mascarpone cheese
1 egg, separated
2 tbsp plain yogurt

2 tbsp superfine sugar
2 tbsp dark rum
2 tbsp cold strong black coffee
8 ladyfingers

2 tbsp grated semisweet
  chocolate

>1 Put the mascarpone cheese, egg yolk, and yogurt in a large bowl and beat together until smooth.

>2 Whip the egg white in a separate bowl until stiff but not dry.

>3 Add the sugar to the whipped egg white, then gently fold into the mascarpone mixture.

>4 Divide half the mixture among 4 sundae glasses.

> **5** Mix together the rum and coffee in a shallow dish.

> **6** Dip the ladyfingers into the rum mixture, break them in half, or into smaller pieces if necessary, and divide among the glasses.

> **7** Stir any remaining coffee mixture into the remaining mascarpone mixture and divide among the glasses.

> **8** Sprinkle with the grated chocolate.

Serve immediately or cover and chill until required.

butterscotch, mango & ginger sundaes

serves 4

ingredients

½ cup dark brown sugar
scant ½ cup dark corn syrup
4 tbsp unsalted butter

scant ½ cup heavy cream
½ tsp vanilla extract
1 large, ripe mango
4 oz/115 g gingersnaps

4 cups vanilla ice cream
2 tbsp coarsely chopped
 almonds, toasted

>1 To make the butterscotch sauce, melt the sugar, corn syrup, and butter in a small pan and simmer for 3 minutes, stirring, until smooth.

>2 Stir in the cream and vanilla extract, then remove from the heat.

>3 Peel and pit the mango and cut into ½-inch/1-cm cubes.

>4 Place the gingersnaps in a plastic bag and crush lightly with a rolling pin.

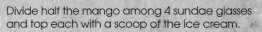

>5 Divide half the mango among 4 sundae glasses and top each with a scoop of the ice cream.

>6 Spoon over a little butterscotch sauce and sprinkle with the crushed cookies. Repeat the layers.

Sprinkle some of the almonds over the top
of each sundae and serve immediately.

caramel pecan apples

serves 4

ingredients
4 tbsp unsalted butter
generous ¼ cup dark brown
  sugar
4 crisp apples, cored and cut
  into wedges
1 tsp ground cinnamon
4 thick slices of brioche
4 tbsp rum or apple juice
¼ cup pecan nuts

>1 Melt the butter in a skillet and stir in the sugar, apples, and cinnamon.

>2 Cook over medium heat, stirring occasionally, for 5–6 minutes, until caramelized and golden.

Spoon the apple mixture on
top of the toasted brioche
and serve immediately.

>**3** Meanwhile, toast the brioche on both
sides until golden.

>**4** Stir the rum and pecan nuts into the pan and
cook for 1 minute.

raspberry croissant desserts

serves 4

ingredients

2 tbsp melted unsalted butter
4 croissants
1⅓ cups fresh raspberries

4 tbsp maple syrup
1½ cups milk
2 extra large eggs, beaten

1 tsp vanilla extract
freshly grated nutmeg,
  for sprinkling

> **1** Preheat the oven to 425°F/220°C. Place a baking sheet on the middle shelf.

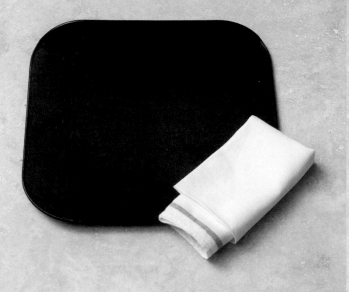

> **2** Brush four 1½-cup ovenproof dishes with half the butter.

> **3** Chop the croissants into bite-size chunks. Mix with the raspberries and divide among the dishes.

> **4** Spoon 1 tablespoon of the maple syrup over the contents of each dish.

>5 Heat the milk until almost boiling, then quickly beat into the eggs and vanilla extract.

>6 Pour the milk mixture evenly over the dishes, pressing the croissants down lightly.

>7 Drizzle with the remaining butter and sprinkle a little nutmeg over each dish.

>8 Put the dishes on the baking sheet and bake in the preheated oven for about 20 minutes, until lightly set.

Serve hot.

ginger baked alaskas
serves 4

ingredients

4 tbsp golden raisins
3 tbsp dark rum

4 slices ginger cake
4 scoops vanilla ice cream or
   rum-and-raisin ice cream

3 egg whites
scant 1 cup granulated or
   superfine sugar

> **1** Preheat the oven to 450°F/230°C. Mix the golden raisins with the rum in a small bowl.

> **2** Place the cake slices, spaced well apart, on a baking sheet.

> **3** Scatter a spoonful of the soaked golden raisins on top of each slice.

> **4** Place a scoop of ice cream in the center of each slice, then transfer to the freezer until solid.

>**5** Meanwhile, whip the egg whites in a large bowl until soft peaks form.

>**6** Gradually whip the sugar into the egg whites, a tablespoonful at a time, until the mixture forms stiff peaks.

>**7** Remove the ice-cream-topped cake slices from the freezer and spoon the meringue over the top, spreading to cover the ice cream completely.

>**8** Bake in the preheated oven for about 5 minutes, until starting to brown.

Serve immediately.

blueberry amaretti desserts

serves 4

ingredients
2¼ cups fresh blueberries
1 tsp almond extract
3 tbsp honey
2½ oz/70 g amaretti cookies,
 plus extra to serve
1¾ cups strained plain yogurt

> **1** Put 1¾ cups of the blueberries into a bowl with the almond extract and 1 tablespoon of the honey. Mash lightly with a fork.

> **2** Crumble the amaretti with your fingers to break up coarsely.

Serve with extra amaretti on the side.

>3 Lightly stir together the mashed berries, amaretti, and yogurt, then spoon into 4 small glasses or dishes.

>4 Top with the remaining blueberries and drizzle over the remaining honey.

plum & almond wraps

makes 4

ingredients

1 sheet (about 11 x 8½ inches/
  28 x 22 cm) prepared and
  rolled puff pastry

¼ cup ground almonds
2 tbsp superfine sugar
½ tsp ground star anise

4 red plums
milk, for brushing

>1 Preheat the oven to 425°F/220°C. Line a baking sheet with baking parchment. Cut the dough into 4 equal-size rectangles, each about 5½ x 4¼ inches/14 x 11 cm.

>2 Stir together the ground almonds, sugar, and anise, then put a tablespoonful in the center of each dough rectangle.

>3 Halve and pit the plums, then cut each into 8 slices.

>4 Arrange the plum slices diagonally across the middle of each dough rectangle, over the almond mixture.

193

>5 Sprinkle any remaining almond mixture over the top, then fold two opposite corners of each dough rectangle over to enclose the plum slices, securing with milk.

>6 Lift onto the prepared baking sheet and brush with milk to glaze. Bake in the preheated oven for 15–20 minutes, until firm and golden.

pear & hazelnut crêpes

serves 4

ingredients
scant 1 cup chocolate
  hazelnut spread
8 store-bought crêpes

4 ripe pears
3 tbsp melted unsalted butter
2 tbsp raw brown sugar

½ cup toasted chopped
  hazelnuts, to serve

> **1** Preheat the broiler to high. Warm the chocolate spread gently in a small saucepan until softened.

> **2** Using a metal spatula, spread each crêpe with a little of the warmed chocolate spread.

> **3** Peel, core, and thinly slice the pears. Arrange the pears over the chocolate spread, then bring the opposite sides of the crêpes over the filling to enclose it.

> **4** Lightly brush an ovenproof dish with a little of the melted butter.

Arrange the crêpes in the dish. Brush with the remaining melted butter and sprinkle with the sugar.

>6 Put the dish under the preheated broiler and cook for 4–5 minutes, until bubbling and lightly browned.

Sprinkle the toasted hazelnuts over the crêpes and serve hot.

no-bake chocolate fudge cake

serves 12

ingredients
8 oz/225 g semisweet
  chocolate, broken into pieces
1 cup unsalted butter
3 tbsp black coffee
¼ cup light brown sugar
a few drops of vanilla extract
8 oz/225 g graham crackers,
  crushed
½ cup raisins
¾ cup chopped walnuts

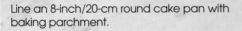

>1 Line an 8-inch/20-cm round cake pan with baking parchment.

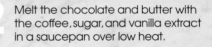

>2 Melt the chocolate and butter with the coffee, sugar, and vanilla extract in a saucepan over low heat.

Turn out and cut into thin slices
to serve.

> **3** Stir in the crackers, raisins, and walnuts and stir well.

> **4** Spoon the mixture into the prepared pan. Transfer to the refrigerator and let set for 1–2 hours.

warm honey muffins with strawberry salsa

serves 6

ingredients
¼ cup unsalted butter,
  plus extra for greasing
1½ cups self-rising flour

1 tsp baking soda
¼ cup honey
scant ¼ cup dark brown sugar
1 egg, beaten

⅔ cup strained plain yogurt
finely grated rind of 1 small
  orange
warmed honey, to glaze

salsa
1¾ cups fresh strawberries
2 tbsp honey
2 tbsp orange juice

>**1** Preheat the oven to 400°F/200°C. Lightly grease six ⅔-cup individual metal pans. Melt the remaining butter.

>**2** Sift the flour and baking soda into a bowl and add the honey, sugar, melted butter, egg, yogurt, and orange rind, mixing lightly.

>**3** Spoon the batter into the pans and bake in the preheated oven for about 20 minutes, until risen, firm, and golden.

>**4** Meanwhile, for the salsa, hull and coarsely chop the strawberries.

203

>5 Warm the honey and orange juice in a small pan, without boiling, then pour over the strawberries and stir lightly.

>6 Remove the muffins from the oven, lift carefully from the pans, and brush the tops with honey to glaze.

Serve the muffins on warmed serving plates with a spoonful of strawberry salsa on the side.

white wine & honey syllabub

serves 4

ingredients
3 tbsp brandy
3 tbsp white wine

2½ cups heavy cream
6 tbsp honey
½ cup slivered almonds

>1 Combine the brandy and wine in a bowl.

>2 Pour the cream into a large bowl and whip until just thickened.

>3 Add the honey to the cream and whip for about 15 seconds.

>4 Pour the brandy-and-wine mixture in a continuous stream into the cream-and-honey mixture, whipping continuously, until the mixture forms soft peaks.

>5 Spoon into serving dishes.

>6 Transfer to the refrigerator and let chill for 2–3 hours.

Scatter over the slivered almonds and serve.

chocolate orange pots

serves 4

ingredients

1 orange
4½ oz/125 g semisweet
   chocolate, broken into pieces
2 tbsp unsalted butter
3 tbsp maple syrup
1 tbsp orange liqueur
generous ½ cup sour cream
strips of orange zest,
   to decorate

>1 Cut the peel and white pith from the orange and lift out the segments, catching the juices in a bowl. Cut the segments into small chunks.

>2 Put the chocolate, butter, maple syrup, and liqueur in a small pan with the reserved orange juices. Heat gently, stirring, until smooth.

Scatter strips of orange zest over the top to serve.

> **3** Stir in 4 tablespoons of the sour cream and the orange chunks.

> **4** Spoon the mixture into serving dishes, then top each with a spoonful of the remaining sour cream.

brandy snaps

makes about 20

ingredients

⅓ cup unsalted butter
scant ½ cup superfine sugar
3 tbsp dark corn syrup

¾ cup all-purpose flour
1 tsp ground ginger
1 tbsp brandy
finely grated rind of ½ lemon

filling

⅔ cup heavy cream
1 tbsp brandy (optional)
1 tbsp confectioners' sugar

> **1** Preheat the oven to 325°F/160°C. Line three large baking sheets with baking parchment.

> **2** Place the butter, superfine sugar, and corn syrup in a saucepan and heat gently over low heat, stirring occasionally, until smooth. Remove from the heat and let cool slightly.

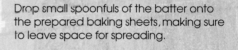

> **3** Sift the flour and ginger into the pan and beat until smooth, then stir in the brandy and lemon rind.

> **4** Drop small spoonfuls of the batter onto the prepared baking sheets, making sure to leave space for spreading.

>5 Place one baking sheet at a time in the preheated oven for 10–12 minutes, or until the snaps are golden brown.

>6 Remove the first baking sheet from the oven. Let cool for about 30 seconds, then lift each snap with a palette knife and wrap around the handle of a wooden spoon. If the snaps become too firm to wrap, return to the oven for about 30 seconds to soften.

>7 When firm, remove the snaps from the spoon handles and finish cooling on a wire rack. Repeat with the remaining snaps, one baking sheet at a time.

>8 For the filling, whip the cream with the brandy, if using, and confectioners' sugar until thick. Chill in the refrigerator until required.

Just before serving, pipe the cream mixture into both ends of each brandy snap.

pineapple dessert

serves 6

ingredients

1 pineapple
2 tbsp raisins
4 tbsp golden raisins

4 tbsp maple syrup
4 tbsp white rum
1 egg yolk
1 tbsp cornstarch

½ tsp vanilla extract
¼ tsp ground ginger
2 egg whites
2 tbsp dark brown sugar

>1 Preheat the oven to 475°F/240°C. Cut off the leafy top and the bottom of the pineapple and discard.

>2 Stand the pineapple upright and slice off the skin. Remove any remaining "eyes" with the tip of a small sharp knife. Cut the pineapple in half lengthwise and cut out the hard woody core, then slice the flesh.

>3 Arrange the pineapple slices in a large ovenproof dish and sprinkle over the raisins and golden raisins. Drizzle with half the maple syrup and half the rum. Bake in the preheated oven for 5 minutes.

>4 Meanwhile, mix the remaining maple syrup and rum with the egg yolk, cornstarch, vanilla extract, and ginger in a bowl.

> **5** Whip the egg whites in a separate bowl until soft peaks form. Stir 2 tablespoons of the egg white into the egg yolk mixture, then fold the remaining egg yolk mixture into the egg whites.

> **6** Spread the topping over the hot pineapple, sprinkle the sugar over the top, and bake in the oven for 5 minutes, or until golden brown.

brown sugar mocha cream desserts

serves 4

ingredients

1¼ cups heavy cream
1 tsp vanilla extract
1¾ cups fresh whole wheat
  breadcrumbs
scant ½ cup dark brown sugar
1 tbsp instant coffee granules
2 tbsp unsweetened cocoa
grated chocolate, to decorate
  (optional)

>1 Whip together the cream and vanilla extract in a large bowl until thick and holding soft peaks.

>2 Mix together the breadcrumbs, sugar, coffee, and cocoa in a separate large bowl.

Remove from the refrigerator and serve.

>3 Layer the breadcrumb mixture with the whipped cream in serving glasses, finishing with a layer of whipped cream. Sprinkle with grated chocolate, if using.

>4 Cover with plastic wrap and chill in the refrigerator for several hours, or overnight.

Index